12 WEEKS

OF *HEALING*

through

CHRIST

12 WEEKS OF HEALING through CHRIST

By: Hitesher Gef

ISBN 978-0-620-72461-6

Published by Free Press Publishers, 30 August 2016

Cover Design by Hitesher Gef

Image on cover by IUrii (Illustrator / Vector Artist, Videographer)

Layout: www.thebook.design

First Print September 2016

For more information on other books, workshops, seminars, prayer, or to contact/book the author:

W www.livebyfaith.co.za | E support@livebyfaith.co.za or info@personalmastery.co.za

W www.personalmastery.co.za | M +2773 429 4857

ALSO BY THE AUTHOR

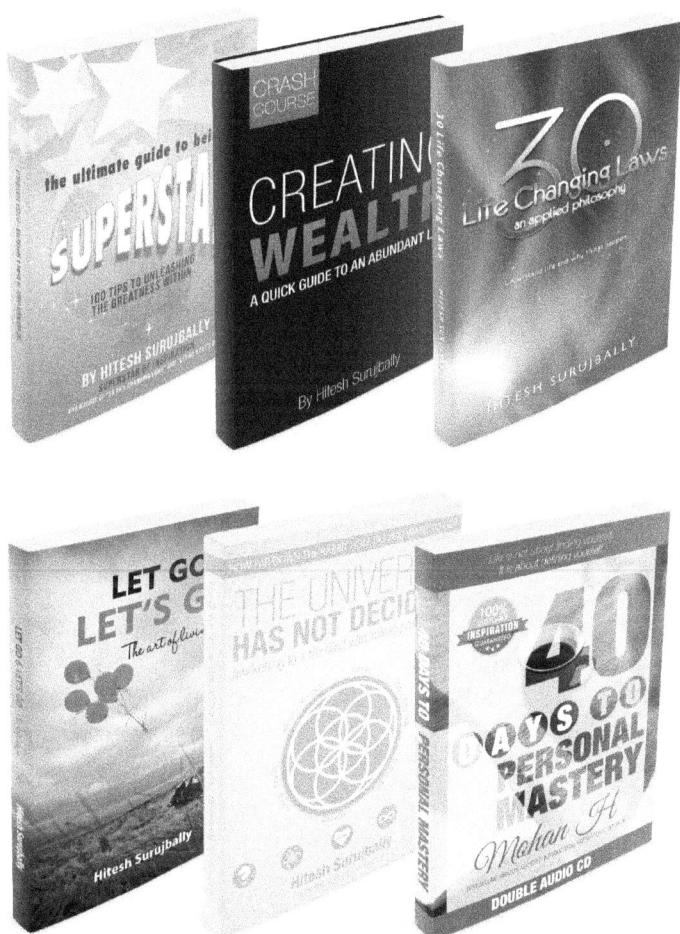

TESTIMONIALS

Hitesher is an amazing, young, inspirational breath of fresh air! He is humble and at the same time powerful, with a passion for transformation!

Sara de Vos

In a world full of darkness, in a world full of pain, some how we always find light, Hitesher is light!

John Dutton

Hitesher's enthusiasm is unstoppable as he guides people masterfully & effortlessly towards a positive mind track of breakthrough clarity of living their greatness.

David Groode

Hitesher is an amazing young man who has incredible insight into life, thus offering extraordinary advice for life's ordinary challenges with great understanding and empathy.

Liz Viviers

Hitesher is a young, enthusiastic dynamic individual that made me remember how great life really is!

Bimal Maharaj

As the anecdote goes, "When the student is ready, the teacher will appear." I stumbled upon Hitesher's first book when I needed to start my healing journey and it has been a constant companion since then. A truly remarkable teacher and author.

Rookaya Vawda

Hitesher is the most amazing and deeply spiritual person I know, he has such wisdom for one so young and has a real gift for teaching others through his creative writing. His books are a must for all who are searching for the truths in life.

Beryl Bazley

If you could harness the power of a raging tornado, dress it in human clothes, you would get Hitesher Gef. Like a Gummi Bear - here, there and everywhere - he bounces around dispensing wisdom, positivity and confidence. Like Paul McCartney said in a song: "Listen to what the man said". You'd be silly not to.

Ravi Govender

What a phenomenal speaker/book writer ! Hitesher`s books & seminars are mindblowing!

Ashveer Kooblal

On first impression you form an opinion that Hitesher is very quiet and shy, until you attend one of his workshops, where he roars like a lion, to get you motivated, pounces on you like a tiger so that you get the point and ultimately wins your heart like a new born pup with his sense of humour.

Besides being a dark horse, he is also a magician, because who else can be in the medical field, an author, a motivational speaker, hold inspirational workshops, create websites, be an actor, and be kind, open, and loving all at the same time.

Chandra Kantha Singh

Hitesher presents Powerful & Practical, Life Changing Wisdom.

Raksha Ramdayal

Hitesher is the "GO TO" guy if you want to be inspired and motivated!

Lubna Nadvi

Hitesher is a soul who cannot be held down or held back – his inner wisdom, and his zest for life and empowering that of those around him is inexhaustible.

Petra Nicol, Consulting Hypnotist

Kingsburgh Child & Family Welfare Society

(NPO No: 002-132)
(PBO No: 930049716)

KINGSBURGH CHILD & FAMILY WELFARE SOCIETY

HELP US MAKE A DIFFERENCE

The Kingsburgh Child and Family Welfare Society is a non-government community based welfare society. Dedicated volunteers and committee members carry out all other fundraising and administrative tasks. Our society is not in receipt of any state subsidy. The society relies heavily on fundraising, donations from the public and business houses as well as community support.

AIMS OF THE SOCIETY

Our primary aim is to protect the interest and promote the welfare of children and families, as well as serve as the avenue of fostering these social and economic forces which safeguard child and family life in the development of resources for the enhancement of their wellbeing.

OBJECTIVES OF THE SOCIETY

Our main objectives are to provide as effective intervention service and to provide direct casework and counselling services to parents and children who have been reported to be abused and neglected; and to empower people (families and individuals) with knowledge and resources to overcome major issues and problems experienced by them, which cause disequilibrium and disharmony. and enable them to utilise these towards improving their quality of life.

WHY WE URGENTLY NEED YOUR HELP

We currently have no funding available to the Society to continue with the important work that we do. We are in dire need of funds to keep our doors open to the community and people that need us. We urgently appeal for your support in any way that may be possible. The Society humbly asks that you please open your hearts to us, and be the miracle that we need. Our contact details are listed below, should you wish to contact us.

CURRENT SERVICES BY THE SOCIETY

The social workers provide a comprehensive social work and supportive service to the community, which includes: Marital Counselling, Material Assistance, Foster Care (screening only), Supervision/Reconstruction Services, Single Parenthood/Unmarried motherhood, Child Abuse and Neglect, HIV Victims (Orphans), Assistance with Grant Applications.

GROUP WORK: COMMUNITY WORK PROGRAMMES

Positive Parenting Programme: Empowers parents in their roles and that they provide the positive parenting that children need. **Victim Empowerment/Domestic Violence:** Uplift people in the community, to enable them to recognise their own strengths, understanding their right's and to enable them to improve the quality of their lives. **Crèche Development Programme:** Enable members of the community to improve the quality of care we provide for our children. **Food Aid Programme:** We provides food hamper for families on a monthly basis, including Christmas. **Child Protection:** Children are taught on how to be safe and they learn about "good touching" and "bad touching". **HIV – Aids Training:** 2-3 day training which focuses on HIV Aids transmission in the immune system, journey of life and understanding children's needs, who are infected and affected by HIV and Aids. **Stress Management Programme:** This program is preventative and is aimed at equipping people with stress management and coping skills, and includes support for apathy, clinical depression, suicidal tendencies, alcoholism and drug dependency. **Educational Workshops:** Awareness programs conducted at the local schools to educate them on the effects of alcohol and drug abuse. **Skills Training and Development:** We provide skill training/ development for client's to be able to contribute financially to their families' income. **Christmas Parties:** Approximately 60 children are spoilt with all the trimmings of a Christmas Party. This includes gifts, refreshments, transport and entertainment.

Address: No.2 Hall Street, Warner Beach, 4126,
Postal Address: P.O. Box 357, Warner Beach, 4140,
Telephone: 031-916 2274,
Fax: 031 916 3007,
Email Address: kingsburghwelfare@telkomsa.net
Facebook: Kingsburgh Welfare – Kingsburgh

This book is dedicated to my mum, dad, brothers, sister in law, my loving family, and my dearest friends. It is only through your love, support, and prayers that I am able to share the story of my healing with the world. Thank you for everything. May my miracle, be a sign that your miracle is on its way. I will always love you.

TABLE OF CONTENTS

PRAISE BE TO GOD

Welcome to the **12 Weeks of Healing through CHRIST** programme.

I wrote this book because I have been so inspired by the love, support, and prayers of my family and friends after I finally decided to have a surgical procedure done. I wanted to document the process of my healing and my return to perfect health and happiness. All of which have been possible with God. I feel like I have been reborn and given a second chance. I will use this opportunity to reach out further to people as I was limited in my ability to do so before. This time, I have all the health, energy and vitality to put into action the purpose that God has placed in my heart.

I have also written this book because I have such a deep connection and affinity with Jesus Christ. I love him so much, and I feel his guiding presence in my life each day.

There is a reason why I chose 12 weeks. 12 weeks equates to approximately 3 months, and new evidence suggests that it takes this amount of time to bring about a permanent change in an individual. I have also chosen 12 because it represents the 12 disciples of Christ. The numbers that make up 12 also add up together to the number of 3, which for me represents the Father, the Son, and the Holy Spirit.

This book is in no way religious but it does have everything to do with God. I believe that religion has everything to do with

God, but God has nothing to do with the religion. We are all united by the one true God, who unites us all. We are all His children, and He is our only Father. I have written this book of healing through the perspective of our Master Healer, Jesus Christ. By this I mean, I have used his words and his work to put together a manuscript that has supported me in my healing, and I know that it will help you in yours.

Extreme care was taken to ensure that the quotes used were translated and transcribed correctly from scripture. I have at times given my interpretation of words spoken by the prophets and Christ. If there are any errors, please send these details to me, to the e-mail provided on the copyright page. My intentions with this book are pure and loving, and I hope that you will read it with love and respect too.

If you belong to the Christian faith, then this book will strengthen your relationship with Christ and give you everything that you need to bring a miracle to your healing. If you are not of Christian faith, then this book will give you a beautiful introduction to the true teachings of Christ and will also help you bring a miracle to your healing. Healing is a very personal thing and requires the mastery of all 12 principles shared in this book. The book itself with all of the words in it will not bring healing. You have to put into practice everything that is shared with you. Be wise to use this book alongside your medical doctor and medication. Never stop or throw away any medicine. Work with God and work with your doctors simultaneously on your road to perfect health. The Egyptians very brilliantly shared that spirit without matter is expressionless, and matter without spirit is motionless. In other words, we are both spiritual and physical beings, and if we are sick, then we have to heal on both levels.

I pray that this book will provide you with the guidance, love, support, and healing that you need so that you can experience the same perfect health as I have. God bless you with health and happiness.

HOW TO USE THIS PROGRAMME

This book should not be read from cover to cover as you would a novel or a self-help book. This book is a healing programme with a duration of 12 weeks. It is divided into 12 sections or chapters. You will start this programme on a Monday and read through each chapter 3 times daily, for that entire week. You will read once in the morning in your mind, once at midday in your mind, and once at night before you sleep, aloud. At the end of each chapter, you will find a record journal which will help you keep track of your healing journey. It also contains a **Thought for the Day**. The purpose of these thoughts is to open your mind and heart for personal transformation. You will find it inspirational, motivational as well as empowering.

By reading one chapter a week, it will take you a total of 12 weeks to complete the book.

Reading in this way means that you will begin to live the words that are being shared with you. The information will move from your conscious mind into your subconscious mind. Once any information goes into the subconscious mind, new habits can be formed, and change will seem to be an automatic process and healing will as well. Your conscious mind is responsible for activities such as walking and talking. Your subconscious mind is responsible for activities such as breathing and making your heart beat. You are unaware of these latter functions and have no control over them. So too with your healing. Healing is a spontaneous and natural occurrence. However, we can support our healing process by using the 12 principles shared in this programme.

If you have any questions or need further guidance, or perhaps even prayer, kindly drop me an email to support@ livebyfaith.co.za

WEEK 1

HEALING BEGINS WITH A HEALING THOUGHT

We are only a single thought away from peace or healing. However, that is much easier said than done. 99% of the problems that human beings face – and I speak of the lucky human beings who have access to basic human needs such as food, shelter, clean water, safety, and health care – are caused by thinking. If you could eliminate thinking, well the excessive kind at least, then we would find ourselves moving into a space of peace and become open to healing. However, this is a mighty challenge as we have more than 60,000 thoughts daily, most of which are repetitive and are just noise between our ears. When we quieten down the mind and move into silence, we have the ability to hear the voice of God, for it is in silence that we make conscious contact with God.

To understand thoughts, we first need to know the source of thoughts. Where do our thoughts come from? Unfortunately, most of our thoughts are not our own. We have borrowed many of our thoughts from our parents, family, the media, books, school, authoritative figures, and religion. Some of these borrowed thoughts serve us and thus lead us to peace and healing and some of these thoughts lead us to pain and suffering. Instead of using the word 'borrowed,' let's call the first type of thoughts **Acquired Thoughts**. The next type of thoughts are **Original Thoughts**. These are thoughts that originate from our mind, through analytical problem solving, deep philosophical thinking or conscious creative thinking. The final type of thoughts are **Inspired Thoughts** which come directly from God. These are thoughts that have entered the minds of great masters and prophets for thousands of years and may have even entered your mind when you make an effort to listen. God is always talking to you, but the problem is that we almost never pay attention.

In order for a thought to be received or given, we need some kind of advanced technological device. We are blessed that God has given this to us. It is called the brain. Your brain is a receiving and transmitting device for thoughts. It works very similarly to that of a radio. You can tune your brain into receiving or transmitting whatever it is that you wish. Your thoughts have the power to create or the power to destroy; it also has the power to heal or the power to hurt. It is, therefore, important that we use this power with great responsibility.

The seed-garden analogy will give you an even clearer comprehension of thoughts. "The mind is a garden, your thoughts are the seeds; you can grow flowers, or you can grow weeds." -Unknown. What would you like to grow in the garden of your mind? Flowers are synonymous with beauty, while weeds are synonymous with chaos. Choose wisely, for the seeds you plant today may be the fruit you have to harvest tomorrow.

For us to fully harness the power of our thoughts, we must further realise that thoughts fall into two categories. Good (positive, Godly) thoughts and Bad (negative, evil) thoughts. It makes it very easy for us to understand this if we visualise the idea of an angel on our right shoulder and the devil on our left shoulder. How do we decipher if the thoughts that we have derived, are from an angel or the devil? It is easier than you may think. In fact, once you become consciously aware of what I am about to share with you, your life will forever be changed. The thoughts that come from the devil are lies. We know that they are lies, as these are thoughts of fear and thoughts that take away your power. These type of thoughts are debilitating in that you will find yourself filled with excuses not to get things done, you will procrastinate, be filled with doubt, and have the false idea that certain things may be impossible or unachievable. The power that I speak of being taken away from you is your power to take the necessary action when required and the power to not be affected by the negative opinions, words or actions of others to you. By constantly listening to the voice of the devil, which are the negative thoughts, you will soon find your life going down on a path of destruction, spiralling out of control. The negative thoughts or the devil, is a liar, and we confirm this when Jesus Christ says, *"When he lies, he speaks his native language, for he is a liar and the father of lies." John 8:44.*

The thoughts that come from the angel will be thoughts of love and power. Power in the form of strength and courage to handle whatever it is that life may throw at you. Love in the sense that you are inspired to do great and good things that serve your community or the world, serve yourself so that you can create a life you truly deserve and most importantly, serve God by doing His work. The thoughts from the angel will therefore, inspire, motivate and empower and fill you with joy, peace and bliss.

As you can see, there is a very clear distinction between the two categories of thoughts. You will know immediately who is feeding you which type of thoughts. The question is, who will you listen to? And who will you obey? *"Resist the devil and he will flee from you." James 4:7.*

A word is singular. Many words that are put together gives you a sentence. A thought is singular. Many thoughts put together becomes a belief. A single thought alone can have very little impact on your life, but when we give attention to that same kind of thought continuously, it transforms into a belief. It is the belief that is responsible for giving you the type of life that you experience. Once a thought becomes a belief it becomes hardwired in your brain, and you will live a life aligned with that belief, whether that belief is a positive one or a negative one. If you have the thought that you will be healed, then this repeated thought over time, will become a belief which means that it will become a truth that you will live. Somehow in some way, beyond your understanding, and by the love of God and His grace, you shall be healed. If you have the thought that you will never be healed that, the same pattern follows as explained above and you will live out that belief that it is factual for you that you may never heal. Healings thoughts which become a healing belief is the key to your healing. We see this so clearly in *Matthew 9:27-28-29 As Jesus passed on his way two blind men followed him with the cry, "Have pity on us, Son of David!" And when he had gone inside the house these two came up to him. "Do you believe I can do it?" he said to them. "Yes, Lord," they replied. Then he touched their eyes, saying, "You have be-lieved, and you will not be disappointed."*

There is a step before the thought can become a belief. While the brain is the receiving and transmitting device, it is the heart that is responsible for creating your experience. When I use the word heart, I do not merely mean it as a figure of speech. Very few people know that the heart has more neurons, which are brains cells, than the brain itself. Furthermore, the heart has a larger electromagnetic impulse than that of your brain. The heart is the seat of all feelings and the brain responds to these feelings by releasing the corresponding protein, which may be a hormone, or a chemical that will result in you "feeling" good or bad in your body which is expressed as laughter and smiles, or tears and depression. It is more evident here in *Proverbs 23:7, "As a man thinketh **in his heart**, so is he."* It does not say "in his brain," it is very clear that it is his heart. Remember that a thought by itself would not have a significant impact on your life. A thought needs to be activated or turned on for it bring about transformation in your life. Most people are not in sync in thought, word and deed. People think one thing, but will utter another, and act out some other thing. This is a false way of living. We are living a lie and are not aligned with God. Jesus was always in sync in thought, word and deed. Whatever it is he thought in his mind, he felt in his heart and actioned out perfectly. This was one way he was able to, through our Father, perform such incredible miracles. Your thought of healing must combine with the feeling of healing; this combination of thought and feeling will activate the process of healing. This process is valid and correct for any thought. I believe that Jesus may have been hinting at this when he said, *"If two of you shall agree on earth as touching anything, it shall be done for them by my father which is in heaven..." Matthew 18:19.* This is further extenuated in *Mark 11:23 "Truly I tell you, if anyone says to this mountain, 'Go, throw yourself into the sea,' and does not doubt in their heart but believes that what they say will happen, it will be done for them."*

To seize all thinking is a nearly impossible task. In fact trying not to think, leads to a thousand more thoughts. Such is the nature of the mind or the beast. So how then does one restrain the mind from thoughts of negativity which deny us peace and healing?

Affirmations are short positive statements that you say either silently or aloud. A powerful example of this in relation to healing would be, "I am healed in the name of Christ." This constant thought will become a belief and therefore become your experience. But remember that unless you feel what you are affirming in your heart, then this thought has no value to you. You can also start the day by dedicating every thought you have to our Father. You can include the following into your morning prayer before you begin your day – "I dedicate every thought, word, and deed to thee, and so let every thought word and deed be pure and good..." This addition to your prayer means that God will support you with your negative thoughts. Each thought you have has the power to be a prayer or a curse and it really is the case, as your thoughts can only be either good or bad. If it is good, it is a prayer, if it is bad, it is a curse. Which are you inviting into your life? Which do you wish for others? God is listening to your thoughts, and nothing escapes Him. Become conscious of God's presence with you daily and never feel bad to ask for love and support when you need it. God wants you to be happy and filled with joy, but He can only rescue you if you reach out to Him and allow him to save you.

HEALTH RECORDER
WEEK 1

Monday   Date: _____   **N° of times**

☐ I have read Chapter 1

☐ I have read the Thought of the Day below

"A person is wise, not based on the knowledge he/she possesses, but by how much that knowledge is shared with the world."

Hitesher Gef

Tuesday   Date: _____   **N° of times**

☐ I have read Chapter 1

☐ I have read the Thought of the Day below

"If only one person supports and loves you, then that is enough, for the entire Universe exists within that one person."

Hitesher Gef

Wednesday Date: _____ **Nº of times**

☐ I have read Chapter 1

☐ I have read the Thought of the Day below

"A person is not rich because of the things they have, but by how quickly he/she gives them away."

Hitesher Gef

Thursday Date: _____ **Nº of times**

☐ I have read Chapter 1

☐ I have read the Thought of the Day below

"To write the greatest life story that has ever been told, you have to discover a treasure far greater than gold."

Hitesher Gef

Friday Date: _____ **Nº of times**

☐ I have read Chapter 1

☐ I have read the Thought of the Day below

"Be as accepting to love, as the ground is to a raindrop, and your entire life will be filled with joy."

Hitesher Gef

WEEK 2

THE POWER OF WORDS

Many centuries ago there was a village that was affected by a sickness that left the children very ill. No matter what medication was given to these poor boys and girls, nothing seemed to help. One day, a saint walked through the village and heard about the pandemic that distressed the community. He went from home to home praying for each child until he eventually found himself praying for children in the streets. Suddenly a voice boomed out from the crowd that had gathered, "Do you really think your prayer can help these kids where medicine had failed!?" The saint immediately lashed out at the man who had spoken and replied cursing, "You stupid fool, you know nothing, go back to where you belong!" The man upon hearing this came forward and was about to punch the saint across his left cheek when the saint put up his hand and smiled very lovingly and said, "If a few words of insult can make you so angry, can kind and caring words not have the influence to heal?" The saint healed more than half the village that day.

This story so perfectly illustrates the power of words. Words and the meaning behind the words have the power to make us or the power to break us. There is a clear difference between words such as, "You are hired! You won $10000! The operation was a success! It's a boy! I love you!" as compared to, "You are fired! You are blacklisted! The operation didn't go as planned! I hate you!" Just reading these words will incite a particular emotion within you.

Politicians around the world use words to win elections, and good leaders use words to bring calm to a nation after a calamity. Some leaders will use words to bring about fear and terror or perhaps cause people to act out violently. It is clear as day that words have power. The question is, are you using this power for good or for evil?

The words you speak daily in your life have an impact on your world and your life. Each word you speak could be healing you or hurting you. *John 1:1 says, "In the beginning was the Word, and the Word was with God, and the Word was God."* Are your words Godly or are they something else?

Matthew 12:34-37 "You serpent's brood, how can you say anything good out of your evil hearts? For a man's words depend on what fills his heart. A good man gives out good - from the goodness stored in his heart; a bad man gives out evil - from his store of evil. I tell you that men will have to answer at the day of judgment for every careless word they utter - for it is your words that will acquit you, and your words that will condemn you."

How do know if your words are Godly? Well, you can easily tell if you follow the 5 Golden Rules of speaking. Before you speak, ask yourself these 5 questions: Is it helpful? Is it necessary? Is it kind? Will it improve upon the silence? Is it true? If you can answer yes to all 5 questions, then whatever you will speak will be Godly. At any given time, never speak to judge, to criticise, to hurt, to insult, to demotivate, to curse and to condemn. Jesus says in *Matthew 7:1-2 "Don't criticise people, and you will not be criticised. For you will be judged by the way you criticise others, and the measure you give will be the measure you receive."* When we read these words spoken by Christ, we always forget to include ourselves into this teaching. We are also "people" too. In fact, it is true that it is not others that we judge and criticise the most, but ourselves. We hurt ourselves more than we do others and fail to see such an obvious truth.

Speaking words of criticism, judgment and such are like throwing hot coals at someone. In the end, it is us that gets burnt. It is like drinking poison and expecting the other person to die. The words we say to others are gifts that will return to us in a form we may not recognize and understand until we read scripture or introspect.

It is true that it is wiser to remain silent than to open your mouth and remove all doubt. We know a man to be a good man by his actions and by his words. Christ repeatedly said that the way to the Kingdom of Heaven was by believing in him, or by believing in his **words** or his works.

We spend much time cleaning our bodies making ourselves look good on the outside. But how much time daily do we take to cleanse our hearts and to cleanse the words we speak? *Matthew 15:10-11 Then he called the crowd to him and said, "Listen, and understand this thoroughly! It is not what goes into a man's mouth that makes him common or unclean. It is what comes out of a man's mouth that makes him unclean."*

Disease and sickness can only exist in a body due to toxicity. Toxins can either be in the form of food or from our environment or numerous other sources. But I also know that negative thoughts and negative words are highly toxic and have no place in the heart or tongue of a person who seeks to heal.

Nikola Tesla said that If we want to understand the secrets of the universe, that we should think in terms of energy, frequency, and vibration. Words are sound energy that have frequency and vibration. Words are sounds! Just like music. When we listen to the hymns at church, we feel a deep connection with God. This is the power of words vibrating through us, and healing us. The challenge is to be in this constant state of grace.

It may seem like quite an impossible task, but it is very simple. Do the following: Follow the 5 Golden Rules to speaking. Commit to 2 days in a week where you will only utter positive words. Keep a reminder on your phone at least once a day to check how you are doing with your words. Once a week meet with friends and family to talk about all the things you are grateful for instead of all the things you can complain about. Commit to a word of God that will say out loudly throughout the day, as you cannot pray and curse at the same time; it is only possible to do one thing at a time!

Know that the words you utter with your lips have the power to heal you and those around you. There are 4 very powerful healing phrases that we can say in almost every moment of our lives. These words are, "I am sorry. Please forgive me. I love you. Thank you." You can find a reason to use these words no matter the circumstance or the time of day.

Prayer can be in the form of words. Let us pray that Our Father cleanses our minds and hearts of hate and sows love in us all. Amen.

HEALTH RECORDER
WEEK 2

Monday   Date: _____   **N° of times**

☐ I have read Chapter 2

☐ I have read the Thought of the Day below

"He who laughs the loudest, lives the longest."

Hitesher Gef

Tuesday   Date: _____   **N° of times**

☐ I have read Chapter 2

☐ I have read the Thought of the Day below

"Sometimes having a little faith, could change your fate."

Hitesher Gef

Wednesday   Date: _____   **Nº of times**

☐ I have read Chapter 2

☐ I have read the Thought of the Day below

"The way a man treats his mother will determine the way the world treats him."

Hitesher Gef

Thursday   Date: _____   **Nº of times**

☐ I have read Chapter 2

☐ I have read the Thought of the Day below

"A loveless heart begets a loveless life. A love full heart begets a love filled life."

Hitesher Gef

Friday   Date: _____   **Nº of times**

☐ I have read Chapter 2

☐ I have read the Thought of the Day below

"Life is not about finding yourself; it is about defining yourself."

Hitesher Gef

WEEK 3

PRAYERS ARE ALWAYS ANSWERED

Many years ago, I read that "God answers all prayers, sometimes the answer is just no." At the time, this served as a perfect answer as to why many of my prayers remained unanswered. However, Christ has confirmed that if we ask for anything in his name, we shall receive it, and he also said that if we believed in our hearts that we would receive what we had asked for, then we would surely receive it.

However, I have always reflected on my life and even reflected upon my reflections and came up with an interesting revelation. It is surely not a new one, and I am certain that you may have had this revelation too. Aren't you glad that many of your prayers were not answered by getting what you asked for? I sure am. This is a fascinating question and requires deep spiritual insight.

I have now come to understand that I, and many other people too, have confused true prayer with some of the following. We sometimes pray but get prayer confused with a **request**. A request is when we ask God for something that we know we either don't want and most certainly don't really need. For example, "Dear God, I would really like buy that new iPhone this year, please make it happen." We sometimes pray but get prayer confused with an **order**. For example, "Dear God, You owe me. Please make sure I get that pair of shoes." We sometimes pray but get prayer confused with **bargaining**. For example, "Dear God, If you help me win the lotto, then I will never miss Sunday service ever." We pray but often get prayer confused with a **favour**. For example, "Dear God, I have never asked for anything before, please make this one thing happen for me." You are most certainly *favoured*, but God will not grant you any favours.

Be honest with yourself, how many times have you made a request, an order, a bargain or a pulled in a favour from God, and have gotten the above confused with a prayer? Now do you actually understand why your prayers were not answered? There is one more item to add to this list, and it is the most common mistaken form of prayer. It is a prayer that is in the form of desperation and begging. The energy from which a prayer is made from desperation and begging is one of fear. In a space of fear, your heart closes, and so does your connection with our Father. Desperation is the opposite of Inspiration. Desperation is also very close to expiration. It is life taking, energy draining, and love depleting. No prayer will ever be answered from this space. When you are begging, you are claiming that you have nothing and denying the truth that has been shared with you that, *"All I have is yours, and all you have is mine. And glory has come to me through them." John 17:10.* All that belongs to our Father belongs to you as well. Yes, I know that in this moment you may feel a lack of finances, you may feel a lack of wellness, you may feel the lack of a partner. But do not make this your truth and your belief. Pray as if all that is rightfully yours is on its way to you and shall be received.

One day, the disciples of Christ made a request to him, *"Teach us to pray." Luke 11:1.* Jesus replied by simply giving them, what we know as The Lord's Prayer. *"Our Father which art in heaven, Hallowed be thy name. Thy kingdom come. Thy will be done on earth, as it is in heaven. Give us this day our daily bread, And forgive us our trespasses, as we forgive, those who trespass against us, And lead us not into temptation, but deliver us from evil. For thine is the kingdom, and the power, and the glory forever, Amen." Matthew 6:9-13*

Consider the simplicity of this prayer. But do we understand this prayer and how powerful it is? We pray but we cease to understand. We offer lip service. We repeat these words every Sunday or perhaps every day, but almost never take the time to know how this prayer can bring healing and every other thing we need into our lives. *"I will pray with the spirit, and I will pray with the understanding also." 1 Corinthians 14:15.*

This prayer is conveying the message that God lives within you, and this God has a holy name. God wants the very best for you, and He will reign in your life, as He reigns in heaven. Live in this present moment, in this day only and each day you will receive whatever you need to live. We ask for forgiveness for ourselves, and for forgiveness for others who may have harmed us. Keep us in the light Lord, and keep the darkness away. You are everything, and we will glorify you forever.

If you connect and meditate on each line in this prayer, you will have no need for another prayer. After all, this is what Christ himself has given to us. However, the beauty of God is that we are never limited to one prayer, and we may pray whatever we feel in our hearts. But we must use the correct method in praying, or our prayers may not be answered.

Firstly let me share with you that you really have no need to pray, for God knows everything in your heart before you can even think it in your mind or speak it with your lips. *"For your heavenly Father knoweth that ye have need of all these things."*

Matthew 6:11. We pray for our benefit, to bring out this strong feeling of belief in order for us to receive. God is standing outside your front door, waiting to give you everything you need, but if you do not open your door, how can your prayer ever be answered? Prayer is the action step that opens the door. *Matthew 7:7-8 "Ask and it will be given to you. Search and you will find. Knock and the door will be opened for you. The one who asks will always receive; the one who is searching will always find, and the door is opened to the man who knocks."*

Here is the method for prayer, to ensure that it is always answered:

Whenever you pray, use the word **command**. Do not confuse the word demand for the word command. To demand is to ask for something forcefully, as if whatever it is you want, does not already rightfully belong to you. You are not taking anything from away from anyone. In fact, you are merely opening your hands and heart to receive. The word command carries an energy that there is no other option but to do what is being asked. There is no doubt that will receive what is being asked. It is called the 10 Commandments, not the 10 *Demandments*. You would thus start your prayer with, "In the name of Christ, I command…."

Remember *Luke 14:9-14? "Have I been such a long time with you,"* returned Jesus, *"without you really knowing me, Philip? The man who has seen me has seen the Father. How can you say, 'Show us the Father'? Do you not believe that I am in the Father, and the Father is in me? The very words I say to you are not my own. It is the Father who lives in me who carries out his work through me. Do you believe me when I say that I am in the Father, and the Father is in me? But if you cannot, then believe me because of what you see me do. I assure you that the man who believes in me will do the same things that I have done, yes, and he will do even greater things than these, for I am going away to the Father. Whatever you ask the Father in my name, I will do - that the Son may bring glory to the Father. And if you ask me anything in my name, I will grant it."*

All prayer should begin with Christ's name, followed by the word command, which is followed by the prayer itself. Here is the full prayer. "In the name of Christ, I command that I am healed." This is the first part of the prayer. You may add to that by extending and colouring that in further, but I assure you that there is no need. However, there are benefits by continuing with your prayer. You see the most important part of prayer is believing. Keep praying until you have a feeling of absolute certainty within you that you will receive that which you have prayed for. Unless you connect with this feeling, your prayer will never be answered. You must "feel" healed, even if every cell in your body is telling you that you are not. Remember that it is the devil on your left shoulder feeding you more lies. Your faith must be bigger than your doubt. The second part of your prayer should be, "Thank you dear Lord. Amen." You must close the prayer by thanking God for answering your prayer. When you say this, you are confirming that your prayer has already been answered. Gratitude is the key that opens up the love in our hearts, and it is this love that is healing energy. For God is Love and Love is God. Allow this healing energy to flow throughout your body. In fact, the shortest prayer in the word is "Thank you." You can do this prayer 24 hours a day, no matter where you are. The more you say this prayer, the more you will find that miracles become a natural occurrence in your life. Once you activate gratitude in your heart, you need to surrender your prayer to God. This will allow God to do His work.

Each prayer should therefore contain the following elements: Ask in Jesus's name. Command. Your actual prayer. Believe. Feel. Gratitude. **Surrender**. Be ready to receive. Never tell God how big your problems are. Tell your problems how big God is. There is nothing that God cannot do and nothing He will not do for you, for He loves you unconditionally.

Any time you speak with love and faith, it is a positive prayer. Anytime you speak with fear and doubt; it is a negative prayer. All prayers will be answered if the words and feeling are in alignment. Be very careful not to be praying negatively!

I sometimes like to add another part to the prayer, which is to say, "May my prayer that is to be answered, be for my highest good and for the good of all." The reason I say this, is because we do not always know what is best for us when we pray. God knows what is best for us. He may not give you exactly what you have prayed for, but He will give you what you need the most or sometimes even better than what you had asked. Further to that, it will be what is best for you, and for those closest to you.

We often pray for ourselves, but I feel that the most beautiful prayer is when we pray for others. One of the most honourable things about this opportunity of being human is serving and loving the other 7 billion people on this planet. I have found again and again, that when we help others get what they want, God somehow finds a way to give us what we want. *Mark 6:27-28 "But I say to all of you who will listen to me: love your enemies, do good to those who hate you, bless those who curse you, and pray for those who treat you badly."* If you are unwell, then take the time to pray daily for other people you know are sick. Each time you support others in healing, you heal on some level as well. When you become selfless and start thinking about other people, you shed your ego and begin to fill with love. Again, I say to you, that it is love that heals. Do whatever you need to do, to feel love at all times.

Never doubt the power of a prayer and the impact it can make in your lives of people, including yours. Sometimes, a simple prayer can re-ignite a flame of hope, and sometimes hope is all that is needed to keep moving forward.

HEALTH RECORDER
WEEK 3

Monday   Date: _____   **N° of times**

☐ I have read Chapter 3
☐ I have read the Thought of the Day below

"You cannot become the best. You can only remember that you are."

Hitesher Gef

Tuesday   Date: _____   **N° of times**

☐ I have read Chapter 3
☐ I have read the Thought of the Day below

"If you believe it can be done, Then half your battle has been won before you have even begun!"

Hitesher Gef

Wednesday   Date: _____   N⁰ **of times** ☐

☐ I have read Chapter 3

☐ I have read the Thought of the Day below

"Your purpose is to be the magnificent being you are. Be that and everything else falls into place."

Hitesher Gef

Thursday   Date: _____   N⁰ **of times** ☐

☐ I have read Chapter 3

☐ I have read the Thought of the Day below

"You have courage because you have strength, you have strength because you have faith."

Hitesher Gef

Friday   Date: _____   N⁰ **of times** ☐

☐ I have read Chapter 3

☐ I have read the Thought of the Day below

"The harshest winter is followed by the most beautiful spring. Whether it is seasons or life. Love... and Spring. Same kind of thing."

Hitesher Gef

WEEK 4

LOVE IS THE ABSENCE OF FEAR

If God is Love, then the Devil is Fear. Love opens hearts; Fear closes hearts. Love finds a way; Fear remains lost. Love never gives up; Fear loses hope before even beginning. Love believes, Fear deceives. Love gives. Fear always takes. Love is kind; Fear is blind. Love sees opportunity; Fears sees adversity.

"There is no fear in love but perfect love casteth out fear: because fear hath torment, He that feareth is not made perfect in love."
1 John 4:18.

Fear is a disease in itself. It is far more crippling than anything I have ever seen. I have heard numerous stories of people climbing Mt. Everest without legs, and I have heard numerous stories of people with legs tell me how they won't attempt to climb Mt. Everest due to some fear. Let's be honest; we all feel fear from time to time. Courage is not the absence of fear; it is staring fear straight in the face and giving it everything you have. Most battles in life are lost because people are afraid to even fight. How can a battle be lost, if you do not give yourself an opportunity to fight? Famous American Hockey player,

Wayne Gretzky said, "You will miss 100% of the shots you do not take." This was exactly the position I was in before I found healing for myself. For almost 6 years, I made a feeble attempt to fight, until one day, I stood up and fought back hard. Today I am happy to be living a perfectly healthy life through the grace of God.

80% of all illness is due to some form of stress. Stress is often the result of either worry, fear or anxiety. All 3 are different variations of the same thing. When we are in a state of fear, we activate the fight or flight response in our bodies. This is a built in defence mechanism which we needed to survive thousands of years ago when we lived in caves. If we saw a dangerous animal such as a lion, adrenalin and cortisol were released into our bloodstream, so we could then choose to either fight the lion or run away from the lion. Adrenalin and cortisol are needed occasionally in real emergency situations in life, such as a man lifting up a car off a boy that is trapped underneath or helping athletes greatly before a race or performers before getting on stage. However, everyday people like you and I rarely find ourselves in these situations, but we still have adrenalin and cortisol running through our system. The result is that our bodies become weakened over time. Our organs do not function optimally, we begin to age prematurely, we cannot think clearly or focus, and we have no energy to live yet alone enjoy life. The end result of this is disease and pain.

The good news is that this can all be reversed. The devil or fear makes things appear far worse than they actually are. For most people, *waiting* to see the dentist is more painful than actually seeing the dentist. Most fears in life almost never happen. Worrying is like a rocking chair, it gives you something to do, but never gets you anywhere. *Psalms 23: 4 "Even though I walk through the darkest valley, I will fear no evil, for you are with me; your rod and your staff, they comfort me."* One of my favourite quotations of all time comes from a book called *A course in Miracles*, which simply states, "If you knew who walked by your side on this path that you have chosen, you would never know fear."

Fear, disease, and darkness can all be reversed with love. If fear is darkness, and love is light, then all we need to eliminate the darkness is to turn on the light. Don't you find it quite comforting to know that all the darkness that fills an entire room could never extinguish the light of a single candle? Isn't it also quite fascinating to learn that the light of a small candle is enough to illuminate an entirely dark room?

When I use the word Love, I am not speaking of the romantic kind. I am talking about pure, unconditional, infinite love. In this beautiful state of love; things like judgement, fear, suffering, guilt, shame, anger, envy, greed, lust, gluttony, and jealousy do not exist. Light is not the opposite of darkness; it is merely the absence of darkness. Love is not the opposite of Fear, it is the absence of Fear. Where there is God, the devil does not exist.

Jesus was once asked which of all the commandments is most important, and we see his reply in *Matthew 13:31-35 When he had gone, Jesus spoke, "Now comes the glory of the Son of Man, and the glory of God in him! If God is glorified through him then God will glorify the Son of Man - and that without delay. Oh, my children, I am with you such a short time! You will look for me, and I have to tell you as I told the Jews, 'Where I am going, you cannot follow.' Now I am giving you a new command - love one another. Just as I have loved you, so you must love one another. This is how all men will know that you are my disciples because you have such love for one another."*

If you are a true follower of Christ, if you honestly claim to be a Christian, then love every person in this world, the same way that Christ loves you. Jesus did not make any mention of race, colour, creed, religion, sex, nationality or any other exceptions to this new commandment. In fact by the practice of this single commandment you encompass all 10 commandments, as everything leads to love, just as everything leads to God.

In order to move into a state of love, we first have to accept ourselves for all we are and all we are not. We need to accept our situation or circumstance. Acceptance means that you trust, which is a bridge that leads to faith and surrender. When we are in a place of acceptance, peace will immediately fill the space inside us. Only when we are in acceptance of ourselves, can we move in accepting others, no matter what they have said to you, and especially more if they have done anything to you. Jesus reiterates it in *Matthew 5:43-45* *"You have heard that it used to be said, "You shall love your neighbour", and 'hate your enemy', but I tell you, Love your enemies, and pray for those who persecute you, so that you may be sons of your Heavenly Father. For he makes the sun rise upon evil men as well as good, and he sends his rain upon honest and dishonest men alike."*

Christ reinforces his message again *in Mark 17:3b-4* *"If your brother offends you, take him to task about it, and if he is sorry, forgive him. Yes, if he wrongs you seven times in one day and turns to you and says, 'I am sorry' seven times, you must forgive him."*

Being a loving person, not only allows you to enter the Kingdom of Heaven but also allows you to experience heaven on earth, in this moment, now!

Love is a gift that has been given to us by our Heavenly Father. However, it is not a gift that we must keep. It must be given away. "A bell is not a bell until you ring it, A song is not a song until you sing it, Love in your heart is not put there to stay, Love isn't love until you give it away." Unknown.

Love is healing energy. Fear is a life stealing energy. Be consciously aware that in any given moment you can choose love, and you can choose health and wellbeing.

HEALTH RECORDER
WEEK 4

Monday   Date: _____   **N° of times**

☐ I have read Chapter 4
☐ I have read the Thought of the Day below

"Love is the answer. What is the question?"

Hitesher Gef

Tuesday   Date: _____   **N° of times**

☐ I have read Chapter 4
☐ I have read the Thought of the Day below

"We may not be able to predict what happens next...We can, however, predict how we feel next."

Hitesher Gef

Wednesday   Date: _____   **Nº of times**

☐ I have read Chapter 4

☐ I have read the Thought of the Day below

"Success is not a choice if failure is not an option."

Hitesher Gef

Thursday   Date: _____   **Nº of times**

☐ I have read Chapter 4

☐ I have read the Thought of the Day below

"Your life is a bestseller. Make sure you don't leave yours unwritten."

Hitesher Gef

Friday   Date: _____   **Nº of times**

☐ I have read Chapter 4

☐ I have read the Thought of the Day below

"May the day that's about to unfold, reveal life's greatest mysteries to you!"

Hitesher Gef

WEEK 5

FAITH IS THE PRECURSOR TO SURRENDER

Andrew decided to a hike up a mountain one Sunday afternoon after lunch. He had done this hike three times already this year. It helps him clear his head. About half way up the mountain, it began to get very foggy, and Andrew was struggling to see. It wasn't very long before he realised that he was lost. He started to panic when the sun began to set with the sky turning dark very quickly. While trying to find his way back through the darkness and the fog, he tripped and found himself rolling down the mountain. He tumbled and bumped every part of his body as he desperately tried to grip onto something. Finally, his hands managed to grasp onto a branch. He looked down and could only see fog. There he was, hanging onto the branch, with his feet dangling in the air. Fear filled his entire body, and out of this fear, he called out in prayer. "God, please help me!" Suddenly a booming voice from out of the heavens shouted back, "My son, let go..." Andrew in disbelief replied to the voice. "God, is that you? Why are you asking me to let go? I will fall to my death if I do. Please help me." The voice again replied, "My son, do not worry, let go." Andrew began to get angry. He started thinking that God had wanted him to die. He did not let go. He held onto the branch even tighter. He continued holding on until the sun began to rise and the fog began to clear. His hands were red and his arms extremely sore from holding onto the branch all night. Andrew was exhausted and could not hold on anymore. He looked below his feet. He was only 5 inches off the ground!

We are all like Andrew. We all think that it is harder to let go than it is to hold on, but the opposite is actually true. Letting go frees us from the pain and suffering that we need not endure. We hold onto our problems, and decide to carry them ourselves. It then becomes heavier and makes the journey of life more miserable. If you have ever travelled, you would know that it is best to travel light. You are traveling through the journey of life, and you should get rid of unnecessary baggage. The more bag-**age** we carry, the more we age, and the closer we are to answering death's call. The real test of our faith is during times of adversity. How many times have we failed in our faith in God? Faith and patience are the same thing. If someone tells you to have faith, they are actually asking you to be patient. If someone is asking you to be patient, they are actually asking you to have faith.

Understand that you cannot have more faith or less faith. It is either you have faith, or you do not. In fact, even if you have faith as small as a mustard seed, that faith is more than enough to do the seemingly impossible. *Matthew 17:20 He replied, "Because you have so little faith. Truly I tell you, if you have faith as small as a mustard seed, you can say to this mountain, 'Move from here to there,' and it will move. Nothing will be impossible for you."* It is not how much faith you have that matters; it is just important that you have faith.

Do you remember the story of Paul, who upon seeing Jesus walking on water, asked Christ if he would allow him to do the same? Jesus being the loving master he was, granted Peter his prayer and so Paul walked on water too. But it wasn't long before Paul doubted and begin to sink into the water, and still Jesus reached out a hand to him. *Matthew 14:31 Immediately Jesus reached out his hand and caught him. "You of little faith,"* *he said, "why did you doubt?"* God can heal us, but our doubt and lack of faith *can* also stop the healing process from taking place. **Complete healing involves all 12 principles explained in this book to take place.** Faith is just one of them. Do not allow anyone to tell you that it is your lack of faith by itself that is keeping you from being healed.

However, faith has the power to heal you if you allow it to. In fact, many times people have thanked Christ for healing them, and his reply would contain one of these 3 statements. 1. It is not I, but my Father in heaven who does this work. 2.Do not tell anyone of what I have done. 3. It is not I that is responsible for your healing, but your faith alone that has healed you. We see clear evidence of this third statement in *Mark 10:52 – "Go on your way then," returned Jesus, "your faith has healed you." And he recovered his sight at once and followed Jesus along the road.*

Faith is not about knowing the way, but knowing that a way will be found. Faith is not having the answers, but knowing that an answer will be revealed. Have such faith that if you had to jump off a mountain, you know, that either a net will appear, or you will learn to fly. *2 Corinthians 5:7 For we live by faith, not by sight.*

How does one learn to have faith? I do not believe that faith can be learned. It can only be developed. My own faith has been strengthened by reading the word of God, or listening to the word of God. *Romans 10:17 "Consequently, faith comes from hearing the message, and the message is heard through the word of Christ.*" My faith has gotten stronger by having a good support structure around me. Being surrounded by other people that have faith in you and your healing is enough to have that faith rub off onto you. You cannot put your hand into a jar of honey without some of the honey sticking to your hand. I have also discovered that reading stories of other people that have gone through whatever I am currently being challenged with and have been victorious in their battles, helps with my faith as well. Above all, there is no harm in praying to God to help with your faith. I know that God will never give me anything that He knows that I cannot handle. So instead of praying, "Dear God, please help me get through this." I would rather pray, "Dear God, give me the strength and faith I need to get through this."

I think it is important for me to share with you at this point something I call Calculated Faith. This means that if you are to make any decision, first calculate your risks and benefits before deciding what to do. Discuss with family and friends, or consult with your life coach or spiritual leader in your community. Keep an open heart and open mind. When it comes to your healing, look at both the medical and spiritual options. Most times, it may be the best to find a perfect balance between the two. Have faith that you have made the best possible decision for yourself. This faith will lead to surrender. In surrender, you completely **Let Go, and Let God** take over.

To surrender is not to *give up*, but to *give in* to God's plan for you. It means you completely accept that God is doing what is best for you, even if it does not seem like it at the time. Remember that to surrender does not mean, that you do nothing. You will be called upon to take inspired action. Inspired action is when you are guided by God to do certain things, and you will just know that it is the perfect thing for you to do. Surrendering is allowing God to work through you. The best way to describe surrender is to use the analogy of the river and the boat. Life is the river, Faith is your boat, any Rocks you may encounter are your Doubts, the Oars you throw overboard because God will make the river flow in the direction that you need, at the pace that is best for you. This is surrender. Your only duty is to get into the boat so that God can take you from point A to point B. *"Casting all your care upon Him; for He careth for you." 1 Peter 5:7*

Mark 16:10-12 The man who is faithful in the little things will be faithful in the big things, and the man who cheats in the little things will cheat in the big things too. So that if you are not fit to be trusted to deal with the wicked wealth of this world, who will trust you with the true riches? And if you are not trustworthy with someone else's property, who will give you property of your own?

HEALTH RECORDER
WEEK 5

Monday   Date: _____   **Nº of times**

☐ I have read Chapter 5
☐ I have read the Thought of the Day below

"Point me to your best friends, and I will write your auto-biography."

Hitesher Gef

Tuesday   Date: _____   **Nº of times**

☐ I have read Chapter 5
☐ I have read the Thought of the Day below

"Dancing and Life, same kind of thing aren't they?"

Wednesday   Date: _____   **N° of times**

☐ I have read Chapter 5

☐ I have read the Thought of the Day below

"If you are waiting to be happy, you will always be waiting."

Hitesher Gef

Thursday   Date: _____   **N° of times**

☐ I have read Chapter 5

☐ I have read the Thought of the Day below

"I asked for a drop. I received an ocean. If only I allowed myself to ask for the ocean."

Hitesher Gef

Friday   Date: _____   **N° of times**

☐ I have read Chapter 5

☐ I have read the Thought of the Day below

"You don't have to be the best. You just have to be you."

Hitesher Gef

WEEK 6

MIRACLES HAPPEN DAILY

The difference between faith and a miracle, is that faith is believing that which you cannot see, and a miracle, is seeing that which you did not believe. *John 20:29 "Is it because you have seen me that you believe?" Jesus said to him. "Happy are those who have never seen me and yet have believed!"* Albert Einstein's advice on miracles and life is something that I live by daily. "There are only two ways to live your life. One as if nothing is a miracle and the other as if everything is." I absolutely choose to live my life by the latter.

Before we can actually invite and experience a miracle in our life, we first have to become aware of the many miracles that have happened in your life and are happening in your life right now. I think the fact that I can see, is a miracle. I can see a sunrise and that is such a miracle. I can hear. I can hear the words "I love you" or listen to a baby laugh, and that is such a miracle. I can speak, and with this voice, I inspire people, that is such a miracle. I can walk, I can breathe, I can think, I can imagine, I can create...the list can go on to fill a book, and all of these are my miracles. What about the miracle of how you just managed to avoid an accident? Or the miracle of when you got fired, but got another job paying double your previous salary? How about the miracle of how you somehow managed to find the money that you needed just in time?

If you cannot be grateful for all of these miracles, what makes you think that you will have more miracles in your life? Be grateful for the miracles you have, and you will have more miracles to be grateful for.

How do we make a miracle happen? Firstly, please understand that miracles are not just reserved for a particular group of special people. We are all deserving of miracles. Each and every one of us. However, in life, we never receive what we deserve, we receive what we *think* we deserve. I have a Golden Rule in life which states 3 things. Never believe everything people tell you. Never believe everything you read. Never believe everything you think. If you have thoroughly studied the chapter on thoughts, you would have a good understanding of that last statement. The first step in experiencing a miracle would be to know that you are deserving of one. This can only be achieved if you let go of any guilt or shame you may be carrying by not judging, condemning or criticizing yourself. We will cover this further in the chapter on forgiveness.

Once you know that you deserve a miracle, you now have your heart and arms opens ready to receive.

Next, it is important that you know that you have the power to create and experience your own miracles just as Christ did. Jesus always shared with his disciples this message we see here in *John 14:12, "Greater works than these shall ye do because I go unto my Father..."*

Know that there is no miracle too big or too small for God. After all, size is relative and perceptive. God is far greater and bigger than anything you could ever imagine and far smaller than anything you can ever imagine too. I know that there is no truer truth than *"...with God all things are possible." Luke 1:37*.

Now that we have our foundation knowledge on manifesting miracles let us now focus on how we can experience them.

I believe the answer to manifesting miracles can be found in *Luke 6:38, "Give, and it shall have given unto you, good measure, pressed down, and shaken together and running, over shall men give into your bosom."* There certainly is no greater joy in the world than giving. Tony Robbins says it so perfectly. "The secret to living is giving." To give does not necessarily mean to open your purse. Sure, if you are in a position to provide financially then give. Many people carry guilt around being wealthy and having an abundance of money. The way I see it, though, is that the more money I have, the more I can share and give it away. To give always means that you open your heart. It is in your giving to someone else, no matter what it is that you are giving, that you are making a miracle happen for you. God has worked through you to help them. When you give, you become God's miracle worker. Do you realise that at the exact moment that you give, you instantaneously receive? What do you receive? You receive a feeling of bliss and joy. Once you begin to give, with the pure intention of just to love and serve, then your own miracle is on its way to you. Remember that you can give your time, love, support, assistance, your presence, kind words, and prayer are just a few things that you can give. It need not be money.

"Each of you should give what you have decided in your heart to give, not reluctantly or under compulsion, for God loves a cheerful giver." 2 Corinthians 9:7

Never give with the intention to receive. Never go out and begin giving, thinking that you are going to get a miracle. You will close all the windows and doors of opportunity and miracles to you. Whatever it is you give with the purest of hearts, shall return to you a thousand fold.

Never count the number of times you have given. I have always said, that if you can count the number of times that you have given, then you have given too little. In fact remember the following each day: If someone does something bad to you, forget what they have done. If someone does something good for you, always remember what they have done. If you do something good for someone, forget what you have done. If you do something bad to someone, always remember what you have done – so that you never make that mistake again. Living this way will keep your soul shining, your heart open and your spirit connected to God.

The next step in creating and experiencing a miracle can be found in *Matthew 6:33, "But seek ye first the Kingdom of God... and all these things shall be added unto you."* Christ has said that the Kingdom of God is within you. Where does God live? Would I be correct to say, in the Kingdom, which is in you? Jesus is asking you first to seek God, and when you do all things shall be given to you. To seek God is to make your way to God, by finding heaven. Heaven need not only be experienced when you leave this body and die. You can experience heaven right now, on earth. I will share with you again, that there are 3 ways in which you can enter the Kingdom of Heaven. 1.Believe in Christ. 2. Believe in his words or his work. 3. Follow the commandments given to you. When you follow the commandments, then you will find God. For only those that do His work will find him. Even if you only follow the new commandment given to you by Jesus, which is to love one another as he has loved you, then a miracle is most definitely guaranteed to you.

One day, a city became flooded due to very heavy rainfall. A man was standing on the top of his roof trying to keep safe. The water was rising, and his place of safety was soon disappearing. He prayed to God to help. There was no one around, and he was really beginning to worry, but he kept on praying.

Soon a man came along in a canoe. "Jump into my canoe and I shall take you higher ground," said the man in the boat. The man on the roof replied, "No, but thank you, God will save me." Next, the Sea Guard came by with a big boat. One of the rescuers on board said, "Take this rope and we shall get you to safety." Again the man replied, "No, but thank you, God will save me." The man soon had water up to his waist, when out of nowhere a helicopter appeared. A ladder dropped down, and a voice called out, "Climb the ladder and we will rescue you!" For the third time, the man replied, "No, but thank you, God will save me." Sadly the man went under water and soon drowned. He found himself in heaven where he came face to face with God. He asked God, "My God, I prayed for you to save me from the flood, why did you not come?" God replied, "My good son, I sent you a canoe, a boat, and a helicopter…"

This is a humorous story but has a very significant message. Do not expect your miracle to come in a way that you have envisioned for yourself. God works in wonderful and mysterious ways. Everything can be a miracle. Even your healing may be in the form of a natural medication, or the meeting of a good prophet who prays for your healing, or the chance finding of a good surgeon on the other end of the world, or the discovery of a book which may contain the exact remedy that you need. Every form of healing has its place and should be respected and as well as given a chance. If you do not keep an open heart and an open mind, you may just miss your miracle just as the man missed his canoe, his boat, and his helicopter.

I know without a doubt, that the miracle you have prayed for is on its way to you and any day now, in divine time, by God's grace you shall receive it. If you have not believed before, then believe now. Cast every negative thought and doubt from your heart and stand with open arms ready to be delivered.

"Hold onto your rope! Heaven is bending low. Your miracle is on its way!" Unknown

HEALTH RECORDER
WEEK 6

Monday   Date: _____ **N° of times** ☐

☐ I have read Chapter 6
☐ I have read the Thought of the Day below

"No one is perfect, but everyone is beautiful."

Hitesher Gef

Tuesday   Date: _____ **N° of times** ☐

☐ I have read Chapter 6
☐ I have read the Thought of the Day below

"BELIEVING is only half of faith. KNOWING is going the distance."

Hitesher Gef

Wednesday   Date: _____   **Nº of times**

☐ I have read Chapter 6

☐ I have read the Thought of the Day below

"I found peace in 2 places. In a still mind and an open heart."

Hitesher Gef

⁓⊰❈⊱⁓

Thursday   Date: _____   **Nº of times**

☐ I have read Chapter 6

☐ I have read the Thought of the Day below

"You cannot make a blind man see; just as you cannot make an angry person see reason."

Hitesher Gef

⁓⊰❈⊱⁓

Friday   Date: _____   **Nº of times**

☐ I have read Chapter 6

☐ I have read the Thought of the Day below

"Only two things are needed for prayer. A sincere heart with gratitude inside."

Hitesher Gef

WEEK 7

GOD HEALS ME

"Doctors may treat, but only God Heals." Unknown. Doctors throughout the world do miraculous work. I am eternally grateful to my team of physicians and other medical personnel who took care of me to bring about my miraculous healing. However, while doctors can achieve great feats like heart transplants, only God can make that heart beat in your body.

The power of God permeates through every cell of your body. Imagine if all the cells in your body had the vibration of Christ in it. You are only alive because of God. Everything you can do, and will do is only possible through the power of God that runs through your body. *"What? Know ye not that your body is the temple of the Holy Ghost which is in you, which ye have of God, and ye are not your own? For ye are bough with a price..."* *1 Corinthians 6:19,20*

Beautiful things happen when you begin to have the understanding that you are not the doer. God is the doer. God makes the sun rise and set, He makes it rain, He makes the flowers bloom in spring, He has made this body that you have, which is the most sophisticated device known to man, and He has breathed life into you so that you can become a conscious human being. If only you allowed yourself to be the instrument, then God will play the most beautiful of symphonies through you! After an enjoyable night out of listening to your favourite band play live, you don't go home and talk about how good the guitar sounded or how fantastic the drums were. You do not speak such strange things. You glorify and give praise to the person who played the instrument, who is the musician. This is the person responsible for making the music. This is why we glorify and praise God, as He is the doer of it all. Only when we decide that we are the doer, that everything goes astray, and life becomes far less than a pleasant and enjoyable experience. Even Christ mentioned, in *John 5:30, "I can of mine own self do nothing..."* Jesus continued to give full credit to our Father who did the miraculous works through him.

I have a beautiful poster on my office wall with this inspiring citation from *Philippians 4:13, "**I can do all things through God who strengthens me.**"* Do you think that it may be possible to allow God to work through you, in the very same way that He worked through Jesus? As I write this, I am reminded of the touching Peace Prayer by Saint Francis of Assisi. "Lord, make me an instrument of Your peace. Where there is hatred, let me sow love; where there is injury, pardon; where there is doubt, faith; where there is despair, hope; where there is darkness, light; where there is sadness, joy. O, Divine Master, grant that I may not so much seek to be consoled as to console; to be understood as to understand; to be loved as to love; For it is in giving that we receive; it is in pardoning that we are pardoned; it is in dying that we are born again to eternal life."

When we allow God to work through us, life does not necessary become easier, but we certainly become stronger. We may not have a comfortable journey, but we will arrive at our destination safely. We may not stop all the tears, but we will find more reasons to smile. We may not be able to stop ourselves from falling, but we may not break any bones. The delightful thing about having God take control of our life is that we can now become the passenger and allow God to be the driver. If life really is a journey, then you could not be in safer hands than with God as your driver.

I have always loved the analogy of God to electricity. Let's imagine that every person on earth is a lightbulb that existed in homes across the planet. Some light bulbs may have a wattage of 60W, while another may have a wattage of 300W. Some may be incandescent bulbs, fluorescent bulbs, or halogen bulbs. Some may be big or some may be smaller in size. But not matter what differences may exist with all of these light bulbs, all work with the flick of a switch as electricity flows through them. Electricity was never invented, it always just existed. No one can touch electricity, but it most certainly exists. It is available in every city across the planet and is not limited to time and space. No one fully understands exactly what electricity is, but we do know that it has the power to turn the darkness into light. The electricity does not judge which light bulb is a good one or a bad one, it illuminates each and every one. However, understand this, which is the most important of all: It does not matter how rare, how expensive or how famous the lightbulb is; it is as good as useless if electricity does not run through it.

If case you did not catch on, you are the lightbulb in this analogy. You have almost no value without God. It is God that allows you to shine in this world. This is such a rare and precious gift and should never be wasted. Your life is a gift that is to be shared with the world, it is not yours to be kept hidden from anyone. Doesn't this give new meaning to *Genesis 1:3* *"And God said, "Let there be light," and there was light."* It is your God-given duty to be a beacon of light for others around you. It is up to you to illuminate the path for those who are lost. Service to others is definitely service to God. *Matthew*

25:40 "And the King will reply, 'I assure you that whatever you did for the humblest of my brothers you did for me."

If you have completely surrendered to God and believe in Him, then *"Did I not tell you," replied Jesus, "that if you believed, you would see the wonder of what God can do?" John 11:40.*

Through our Father in heaven, Jesus has healed the sick, brought the dead back to life, given sight to the blind, helped the cripple walk, gave hearing to the deaf, healed a man from leprosy and much more. Do you think that whatever illness you have cannot be healed through the love that God has for you? *Matthew 15:28 "You certainly don't lack faith," returned Jesus, "it shall be as you wish." And at that moment her daughter was cured.*

There are 3 levels of belief. 1. Belief in God. 2. Belief in yourself. 3. Belief that your healing is possible through God. All 3 levels of belief must be activated for healing to take place. Know that God is omnipotent, omniscient, omnipresent. Which means, He is all-powerful, all-knowing, and present everywhere regardless of time and space. So when I say that you should believe that your healing is possible through God; what this really means is God can use any person, medication, or remedy to find healing for you. Begin to practice that you see God in everyone and feel God in everything.

Keep an open connection with God and you shall be guided and guarded in every moment. You are loved for all you are, and all you are not. You are loved for all you have done and all you have not done. You are loved for all you have said and all you have not said. You are loved for who you are, and who you are not. And it is because you are loved, that you are healed; if you believe it to be true.

Do you believe?

HEALTH RECORDER
WEEK 7

Monday   Date: _____ **Nº of times** [ ]

☐ I have read Chapter 7
☐ I have read the Thought of the Day below

"Love can never be owned; it can only be shared."

Hitesher Gef

Tuesday   Date: _____ **Nº of times** [ ]

☐ I have read Chapter 7
☐ I have read the Thought of the Day below

"The source of all pain is in forgetting that God stands beside you."

Hitesher Gef

Wednesday   Date: _____ **N° of times**

☐ I have read Chapter 7

☐ I have read the Thought of the Day below

"Love is one. How we perceive and receive it is many."

Hitesher Gef

———— ❧ ————

Thursday   Date: _____ **N° of times**

☐ I have read Chapter 7

☐ I have read the Thought of the Day below

"I cannot see the end, but I'm on my way."

Hitesher Gef

———— ❧ ————

Friday   Date: _____ **N° of times**

☐ I have read Chapter 7

☐ I have read the Thought of the Day below

"You can either be right, or you can either be at peace. Not both. Choose wisely."

Hitesher Gef

WEEK 8

PERFECT HEALTH IS MY RIGHT

When did the state of your health become less than ideal or perfect? I believe that earth was a paradise where everything was once perfect. It's important that we are careful when we use the word perfect. What may be perfect for one, may be imperfect for another. We also need to bring into this definition of perfection, different situational, social, philosophical, moral and ethical perspectives. So to keep it simple and so that we are all on the same page; I use the word perfect in this context, as having the experience of peace, love, and bliss.

So, as I said above, I do believe that earth was a paradise where everything was perfect in that there was peace, love, and bliss in every moment. However, this was lost at the moment of the "Original Sin" which we know as temptation. This temptation led to the development of three feelings; fear, guilt, and shame, which are the root of the 7 deadly sins; lust, gluttony, greed, envy, wrath, pride, and laziness. It is these vices that disconnected us and thus created the illusion of being separated from God and which led to us being metaphorically kicked out of paradise.

Peace, love, bliss as well as faith and the like, are not physical elements in the sense that they cannot be seen or touched. It can only be experienced within. Anyone who has peace, love, bliss and faith within themselves, will experience near perfect health. This is to say that the invisible elements that exist within you, give rise to the tangible element that we know as the body. In other words, there is a cause and an effect.

This was when your health became less than perfect. The moment fear, guilt, and shame overshadowed the peace, love, bliss and faith within you, you began to experience disease. I am purposely not discussing genetics, the mother's health, drug abuse during pregnancy of both parents, stress and physical trauma to the baby while in the womb. I want to acknowledge these factors, but this is not the topic of discussion in this book.

"Behold, I give unto you power...over all the power of the enemy: and nothing shall by any means hurt you." I am sharing this with you from *Luke 10:19*, because when Christ speaks here, the enemy he is speaking of is the devil. No one has seen the devil, but the devil can come in many forms. In this case, he has come as the enemy in the form of fear, guilt, and shame. The good news is that Jesus also shares that he has given us the power such that we shall not be harmed.

Luke 8:31-32 So Jesus said to the Jews who believed in him, "If you are faithful to what I have said, you are truly my disciples. And you will know the truth, and the truth will set you free!"

This power and truth that He speaks of are Love and Faith. The shackles of fear, guilt, and shame have kept us trapped for far too long. It is now time that we set ourselves free. Jesus has given us the keys, yet we keep ourselves prisoner and experience a life of pain, suffering, and disease.

Imagine that you are driving on the freeway in the afternoon, and the sky soon began to darken. If you did not turn the headlights on, the result would surely be quite fatal to you and other drivers as well. By switching on the lights, we can see the road ahead of us and therefore steer clear of danger, and also keep on the path that will take us to our destination. The light allows us to become aware of our surroundings and take corrective action. The light given to us by Christ are all of his pearls of wisdom. When he spoke, he did not just speak to educate us. He spoke to enlighten us. Each word he spoke is meant to bring us to an awareness so that we may awaken and become conscious loving beings so that we may find our way back home to our Father.

We sometimes forget that we are spiritual as well as physical beings. We shower daily to remove dirt from our body externally, but what do we do to cleanse spiritually? Our spirit becomes contaminated with toxins also. If a tree is bearing bad fruit, you will not try to fix the fruit. You will look for any infection or damage to the root of the tree. You would literally, get to the root of the problem. Your body is the fruit, and it is vital that we remove all toxins that exist at the root level, so we don't have a return of disease or illness.

What are these toxins and where do they come from? Do you remember we spoke about good thoughts and evil thoughts in Chapter 1? Well, the very same principle applies to emotions as well. Some emotions can be healthy (delightful, excited, respectful, worthy, happy), while others can be extremely toxic (anxious, bitter, angry, sad, hateful, resentful). An emotion is essentially an emot-**ion**. An ion is an atom or molecule with a net electric charge due to the loss or gain of one or more electrons. In other words, it may be either positive or negative in nature. The more negative emot-ions you have in your system, the more negative/sick you will become. The more positive emot-ions you have in your system, the more positive/healthier you will become. However, I must stress at this point, that the key to perfect health and wellness is in the balance of these emotions. There is a flip side to being too positive, in that you sometimes reject reality and live in a fantasy world, which can lead to many disappointments. The key is not to be emotional. An emotional person is up one moment and then down the next, and continues with this cycle, which can become rather exhausting. Instead of being emotional we should strive to be balanced and non-reactive. It is better to be pro-active with dealing with life's challenges. If something negative happens to you, stop, take a breather, clear you head, take corrective action, and speak to someone or seek advice. In a non-emotional state, you feel what I call the **God Emotions**, which have no charge at all, and are completely neutral. These are love, peace, bliss, joy, contentment, and gratitude. In these states, you are connected to God, and can think with absolute clarity and are guided by our Heavenly Father.

Negative emotions can get trapped at a cellular level and will remain there until they are dissolved by feeling positive emotions, or by feeling any of the God Emotions. Once a negative emotion is trapped in a cell, it will remain in newer cells when those cells multiply. This means, that if you do not transform the way you think, believe and feel, then you will continue to create more of the diseased cells in your body. Do you know that every 7 years you have an entirely new set of organs, including skin and hair? What I am saying here is that this body that you have now is not the body you had 7 years ago. But if you get a new body then why do you still get sick? Well, as I have explained, when your body was creating new cells to create a new organ, it multiplied with that toxic emotion inside it.

True healing must be holistic. It must involve body, mind, and spirit. You cannot just heal on one level. If you heal the body, you must also heal spiritually and emotionally for you to experience total wellness.

So how do you begin to feel more positive emotions? I will cover more of this in the chapter on forgiveness, but let's commence with the most obvious way. Do what makes you happy. Instead of living a life according to what others expect of you, do what makes your heart sing. Just doing this is enough to lift your spirits and obliterate negativity. Next, stop taking other people's opinion about you seriously. If you listened to everything people said, and took it to heart, you will become a very toxic person. The third thing you should do is not take life so seriously. Be responsible, but don't be so serious. Laugh more, find the light side to your challenges. When you learn to laugh at your problems, then you become a master of life and can handle anything life throws your way.

HEALTH RECORDER
WEEK 8

Monday   Date: _____   **Nº of times** [ ]

[ ] I have read Chapter 8
[ ] I have read the Thought of the Day below

"The world is a reflection of the love in your heart."

Hitesher Gef

Tuesday   Date: _____   **Nº of times** [ ]

[ ] I have read Chapter 8
[ ] I have read the Thought of the Day below

"Faith, not time, will determine when you get what you want."

Wednesday   Date: _____   **Nº of times**

☐ I have read Chapter 8

☐ I have read the Thought of the Day below

"Take off your shoes and walk bare feet today. Let your feet kiss the earth."

Hitesher Gef

Thursday   Date: _____ . **Nº of times**

☐ I have read Chapter 8

☐ I have read the Thought of the Day below

"God...like Love, may not always be seen or felt. But does not mean it's not present in the heart."

Hitesher Gef

Friday   Date: _____   **Nº of times**

☐ I have read Chapter 8

☐ I have read the Thought of the Day below

"Change does not mean you lose anything. It means you transform something."

Hitesher Gef

WEEK 9

BE A WARRIOR, NOT A WORRIER

The first thing I had said to a friend when I was out of the hospital was, "Over the last two weeks, I have been through hell, I have fought the devil, and I have won! I am a soldier of God!"

Isaiah 54:17 "No weapon formed against you shall prosper..." It took me almost six years of living in fear before I had decided to move forward and have my surgical procedure done. The moment I had surrendered to God and let Him take care of me, everything happened so perfectly and naturally. This included finding one of the best surgeons in the world, and one of the most reputable hospitals in my country. I also had the support and love I needed around me, and the most caring medical team that made sure I was comfortable and happy whether I was in the ICU or the General Surgical Ward. I have to share with you that my doctor was truly amazed at my recovery and at how fast I was healing. He mentioned that he had seen a few cases like me, where the patient is undeniably determined to be well, and so they recover quickly. There isn't a scientific explanation as to why this happens. My opinion is that it is simply about having a rock solid armour of faith!

Today I am delighted to share with you that I am in perfect health and am enjoying being reborn and rejoice been given this new life with new energy to be a catalyst for the transformation and healing in the lives of the people of the world.

The week before my operation, I found myself becoming stronger and stronger. There was no doubt that the devil did whisper into my ear words of fear and doubt, but those were drowned out by words of love and encouragement. I knew that I had God by my side and with that all things were possible. *"If God is for us, who can be against us?" Romans 8:13.*

I believe that God has bestowed upon us many powers. One of those powers is the power of choice. Each and every day is **Choose-Day**. From the moment we wake up, to the time we go to sleep, we can choose how we think and feel. We can choose to help or choose to hurt; choose to love or choose to fear; choose to act or procrastinate; choose to heal or remain sick; choose to pray or curse; choose to try or fail to try; choose to push harder or quit; choose to give or always take; choose to support or criticise; choose to accept or judge; and most importantly choose to be a WORRIER or to be a WARRIOR.

In that final statement, I choose to be a warrior (of God). To be a warrior does not mean that you must act out in a violent way. I do not condone violence in any form, whether it is in thought, word or deed, or whether it is against women, men, children or animals. Let me define for you what I mean by warrior and worrier. A *worrier* is someone who lives in fear, is weakened daily by negative thoughts, and loses all hope for things to change for them. A worrier will entertain the devil, the negative words, until they are zapped of energy and life force. I have been a worrier and am in no way judging those who currently identify with this title. From time to time we all fall. There is nothing wrong with falling, but there is something wrong with staying down. If you notice a worrier in your life, then give them the love and support that they need. If you are the worrier, in this case, reach out for love and support. This is the first step in transitioning from being a worrier to a warrior. *Warriors* have a strong support structure around them and are not afraid to ask for help when they need it. Life is not meant to be lived in isolation and total independence. If this were the case, then you would be the only person alive. There is a reason that there are 7 billion people on this planet. It is not a sign of weakness to ask for help; it is a sign that the ego (the devil as well), is losing his grip on you. Warriors fight their inner demons too and reclaim their God-given powers that had been taken away from them in their time of weakness. If you keep getting up each time that you fall, you will eventually tire the devil out. The devil is impatient and will flee when he can no longer break you down.

Do you know any of the weapons that have been bestowed upon you? The weapons that God has given you are: *the power of the measure of faith (Romans 12:3), the power to love and the power to hope (1 Corinthians 13:13), the power not to fear and to believe (2 Timothy 1:7), and wisdom to know that you are the not the devil's property but, God's (1 Corinthians 6:19).*

I think of faith as the armour of my spirit. This armour can only be pierced by doubt and fear. Remember that you will rise by your faith or you will fall by your fear. As long as you have your armour of faith, then no person or thing can stand in your way of success in your work/business or success in your health. The old anecdote that *time heals everything* is untrue. Time does not heal at all. Time does two things. It buries things so deep that you think that you are healed and, we give time undue credit for healing when it is truly you that has just taken a longer period to let go and step into love, thus creating the illusion of time healing. Love, and not time, heals everything. This is why Christ gave us the new commandant to love one another as he has loved us. This is the Golden Ticket to the Kingdom of Heaven and uniting with God. It is love. Where there is love, there is hope and where there is hope, you will find your way to God. As long as you have hope within you, then you have everything. Hope is the first step in what I call the Hierarchy of Infinite Possibilities. Hope leads to believing, which leads to faith, which takes you into love. In the state of Love, God's presence is felt, and all things are possible.

Stepping into power is not a bad thing. This is self-em**power**-ment. You are not using your power to control or manipulate anyone or to hurt and abuse. You become a powerful human being who can positively influence yourself and other people, to be the best that they can be. The moment we give our power away to another person or even an organisation, then they will easily use that power against us. Where power can work against us, when we develop a love for power and move away from having the power to love.

To help you quickly identify whether you are in a worrier state or a warrior state, I have listed a few characteristics below for you.

Worrier: ordinary, thinks within limitations, loses hope, easily gives up, lives in isolation, always anxious. Focuses on the future, puts others happiness before theirs, heart and mind are closed, lacks focus and clarity, prays out of fear and desperation, finds it difficult to sleep, blames people and the world for their problems, doubts the power of God.

Warrior: extraordinary, thinks that anything is possible, has a heart filled with hope, never quits, is open to support and gives support, is in a space of peace, focuses on the present moment, puts their happiness before others, heart and mind are always open, has crystal clear clarity and focus, prays out of love and gratitude, enjoys a good night's sleep, takes responsibility for their life, has faith and believes in the power of God.

Are you a worrier or a warrior? You can choose!

HEALTH RECORDER
WEEK 9

Monday   Date: _____   **Nº of times**

☐ I have read Chapter 9

☐ I have read the Thought of the Day below

"If life was a buffet and the menu was love, make sure today you indulge until you can eat no more."

Hitesher Gef

Tuesday   Date: _____   **Nº of times**

☐ I have read Chapter 9

☐ I have read the Thought of the Day below

"In order to live a life of abundance you have to do the abun-dance."

Hitesher Gef

Wednesday   Date: _____   **N° of times**

☐ I have read Chapter 9

☐ I have read the Thought of the Day below

"I see you. I see me. I see all as divinity."

Hitesher Gef

Thursday   Date: _____   **N° of times**

☐ I have read Chapter 9

☐ I have read the Thought of the Day below

"Be in a place, where there is no space between you and God's grace."

Hitesher Gef

Friday   Date: _____   **N° of times**

☐ I have read Chapter 9

☐ I have read the Thought of the Day below

"Emotion creates commotion. So be still and allow God's will."

Hitesher Gef

WEEK 10

GOD IS WITH ME ALWAYS, IN ALL WAYS

I remember what it was like in school to hang out with my best friend. The world was our playground, and we could do anything as long as we had each other for support. On days that he was sick, it seemed like the worst day in the world. I had felt an emptiness inside but was filled with joy to see him the next day. We all loved weekends, but weekends were two days that I would not see my best friend. Do you have memories of these thoughts and feelings from school?

I like to think of God as my best friend. *"Know that we are in him." 1 John 2:5.* I find peace knowing that I am in God, and God is in me. *"Peace, be still..." Mark 4:39.* The only difference is that with God, He will never leave my side. He is with me at all times.

I grew up listening to the Footprints in the Sand poem by Mary Stevenson. It tells the story of a dream she had one night of God and her walking together on the beach. For each moment in her life, she noticed two sets of footprints on the sand. However, she got quite worried when she noticed during times of trouble, there was only one set of footprints in the sand, and she assumed that they were hers. So she turned to God and asked, "My Lord, why did you abandon me in the times I had needed you the most?" To which God replied, "My child, I did not leave you. It was in those times of distress that I carried you, and that is why you see only one set of footprints."

I am going to share with you now a verse from scripture that allows me to go to bed at night and enjoy a peaceful night's sleep. *"This is what the LORD says to you: Do not be afraid or discouraged because of this vast army. For the battle is not yours, but God's." 2 Chronicles 20:15*

Psalms 55:22 "Cast thy burden upon the LORD, and He shall sustain thee…" Hand over all your worries, concerns, troubles, and challenges over to God and let Him take care of them for you. Instead of you fighting all of your battles, allow God to fight them for you. You have the most powerful, most merciful, most loving and most supreme God by your side who transcends time and space and can do the most incredible, miraculous and seemingly impossible feats. The hardest thing to do sometimes is to step out of the way and allow God to do His work in your life.

Why is it that in times of trouble, we try to figure a way out ourselves before we lose all hope and then turn to God. *"I call on the LORD in my distress, and he answers me." Psalm 120:1.* A wiser way to do it is to hand over the problem to God first and then work on finding a solution. The best solution will come to you from God, via what is known as inspiration. The word inspiration comes from the words **in spirit**, which is translated into **in-God**. In moments of inspiration know that God is working through you. If I ever have to choose between my way or God's way, I would rather choose God's way. I know that God will do what is best for me always in all ways. God knows my past, my present, and my future and knows things I do not. I unconditionally surrender to His wisdom and guidance, knowing very well that God has a beautiful plan for me. *Jeremiah 29:11 For I know the plans I have for you," declares the Lord, "plans to prosper you and not to harm you, plans to give you hope and a future.*

It is so easy to give into fear especially when you are sick and need to go into hospital and have test's done, as well be poked and probed. Most times, you only see family during the designated visiting hours, and so you have to go through everything by yourself. Of course, the devil on your shoulder will give you a thousand reasons to worry and become anxious. However, in those times I remember, *Psalms 118:6 "The Lord is for me; so I will have no fear."* In those moments I know that I am in fact not alone. I have God right here by my side. I see every nurse as God, and every doctor as God, I see every test that needs to be done, as a battle that God is fighting for me and I know that I am protected and safe at all times.

The idea and thought that God is with you at all times will totally eliminate fear from your system. I have used this before giving a speech, or going in for a job interview, or before closing a sale with a client, or when I need to resolve a problem with customer service, or when I need to travel safely at night, or in any other situation you can imagine. There are no limits.

God is there for you and with you at all times, but you have to do your part too. I like the story of the gentleman who prayed to God to win the lottery. (I do not support gambling, but listen to this humorous story) He prayed week in and week out, until months went by. He still never won the lottery. One day he called out very loudly to God at the top of his voice, "God why have you not helped me win the lottery!?" A voice came back, "Would you at least help me out by buying a lottery ticket?" God will help you if you show some initiative to support and help yourself. Pray for your safety at night, but lock your doors. Pray for a safe journey when travelling, but buckle up when driving. Pray to pass your exam, but make sure you study well. Remember that God is not there to work **for** you, but God will work **with** you. It is so important that you understand this. You and God make a powerful team, and you, together with God, can make the impossible, possible. *"So do not fear, for I am with you; do not be dismayed, for I am your God. I will strengthen you and help you; I will uphold you with my righteous right hand."* Isaiah 41:10.

God has always provided, and I know that He will provide more than I have asked and have prayed. I prayed for a flower, and God gave me a garden. I prayed for a glass of water, and God gave me an ocean. I pray for a job, and God gave me a business. I prayed for a car, and God sent me a chauffeur. I prayed for food, and God sent me a buffet. How great and glorious is God? *"Teaching them to observe all that I have commanded you. And behold, I am with you always, to the end of the age."* Matthew 28:20.

I want to close this chapter with a poem that I keep in my left coat pocket, by an unknown author. I invite you to do the same. Read it many times and you will be humbled and transformed by the message.

I asked for strength, and God gave me difficulties to make me strong.

I asked for wisdom, and God gave me problems to solve. I asked for prosperity, and God gave me brawn and brains to work.

I asked for courage, and God gave me dangers to overcome. I asked for patience, and God placed me in situations where I was forced to wait.

I asked for love, and God gave me troubled people to help.

I asked for favours, and God gave me opportunities.

I received nothing I wanted but received everything I needed. My prayers have all been answered.

HEALTH RECORDER
WEEK 10

Monday   Date: _____   **N° of times**

☐ I have read Chapter 10
☐ I have read the Thought of the Day below

"All out of luck? Create your own!"

Hitesher Gef

Tuesday   Date: _____   **N° of times**

☐ I have read Chapter 10
☐ I have read the Thought of the Day below

"The shortest distance between you and I is Love."

Hitesher Gef

Wednesday   Date: _____   **N° of times** [ ]

☐ I have read Chapter 10
☐ I have read the Thought of the Day below

"Let it go. Let it be. Let it flow."

Hitesher Gef

———— ✦ ————

Thursday   Date: _____   **N° of times** [ ]

☐ I have read Chapter 10
☐ I have read the Thought of the Day below

"Love is the flower that blooms in every season."

Hitesher Gef

———— ✦ ————

Friday   Date: _____   **N° of times** [ ]

☐ I have read Chapter 10
☐ I have read the Thought of the Day below

"The only thing in life that you know, is that you really don't know."

Hitesher Gef

WEEK 11

FORGIVENESS IS THE KEY

This is by far the most important chapter in this book and may solely be the reason for your healing. The reason I say this is because I have studied every word of Christ that has been made available to me and I can tell you the word forgiveness is used by Christ more than any other word. There are times when Jesus would not even pray for anyone or even touch them for that matter and healing would take place. He would simply utter the words, "You are forgiven…" and they would be healed.

Why is forgiveness so important when it comes to healing? First, let's understand what forgiveness is. Most people do not take the time to decipher words and to understand what they fundamentally mean. The word for**give**, contains a keyword that tells us what this word is all about. To forgive is to give yourself permission to let go. To forgive is to give yourself permission to have peace of mind. To forgive is to give yourself permission to be free.

Forgiveness has nothing to do with the other person and everything to do with us. We forgive for us. When we forgive, it does not mean we are okay with what the other person has said or done to us. It only means, we no longer hold onto whatever was said and done, so that we can move ahead with our lives. I feel that unless we forgive, it is like a big brick wall that has planted itself on your path rendering you completely stuck. It is so high that you cannot climb over it, so wide that you cannot even go around it and so deep that you cannot even go under it. The only way is through it, and the only way through it, is by forgiving.

Having worked with thousands of people over the past decade, I can tell you that in almost all cases it is seldom that we need to forgive other people. I have found that it is actually ourselves we need to forgive!

Forgiveness always involves something that was said or not said or something that was done or not done. It may include you, another person, an organisation, a country and even sometimes a thing or a concept. There are two main emotions that go with forgiveness. They are guilt and shame. These are very similar emotions. However, you can feel guilty on its own, but if you feel shame, then you also feel guilty as well. Guilt is when you have said or done something that you regret, and you want to be forgiven for these actions. Shame is the same definition as above, but now you would rather allow yourself to feel bad as punishment for doing something, and so you will find yourself sabotaging your life by spoiling relationships or hurting your business. Guilt and shame are dark emotions and can make you really ill.

No matter what you have done or said, or not for that matter, know that you are forgiven. When people came to Jesus for healing, he was aware that they carried guilt and shame within them, and he naturally said to them, "You are forgiven." Jesus did not ask them to tell him the story of what they had said and done which lead to a 1-hour consult so that he could decide if they were worthy of healing or not. No, this never happened. They were forgiven regardless. How merciful is God? It is us that hold onto judgement of others and ourselves. But we forget what has been taught to us. *"For in the same way you judge others, you will be judged, and with the measure you use, it will be measured to you."* Matthew 7:2. Know in this moment that you are forgiven. It is harder to forgive ourselves than it is to forgive others. This is why the greatest enemy is our own selves, and the greatest battle is in our own mind.

Guilt and shame keep us in the past. We live there and lose all the joy and happiness that this present moment has to offer us. Fear on the other side, keeps us living in the future, and has the same outcome as guilt and shame. Guilt, shame, and fear will tire you out. A little child will have boundless energy because they have no concern over the past or future and are filled with love and joy, but an adult will be tired out by the end of a *typical* day at work. This is because we have spent most of our time living in the past or future. When we live in the present; when we are acutely aware of what is happening now and put our focus in this moment then we step into the feeling of love. This love is what connects you to God. This is why Jesus says, *"Unless you change and become like little children, you will not enter the Kingdom of Heaven."* Matthew 18:3.

"Don't worry at all then about tomorrow. Tomorrow can take care of itself! One day's trouble is enough for one day." Matthew 6:34

When it comes to forgiving others, there are two primary emotions. These are anger and resentment. I know what it is like to be cheated on, lied to, insulted, belittled, criticised, used, abused, mistreated, disrespected, shamed, hurt, as well as ignored. I am certain you can add to this already long list. However the more we hold onto the anger and the resentment the more it hurts us. I have always shared with people that anytime you feel any strong emotion with someone then you are in fact involved in a very intimate relationship with them. Some relationships can be inspiring and uplifting where love is experienced and expressed; and some relationships can be toxic where hate, anger, and resentment are experienced and expressed. So if you are in a relationship, there is a chain that connects your heart to theirs. If you are in a relationship that you want, then the chain is just there to keep you two together. However, if it is a relationship that you do not want, then the chain tightens harder and faster around your heart and begins to bleed you as well as drain you of your life. So I want to invite you to release that chain or cut off the chain that is attaching you to this other person. Know that it is you that is holding onto them and that at any moment, you so choose to let them go. *"If your brother offends you, take him to task about it, and if he is sorry, forgive him. Yes, if he wrongs you seven times in one day and turns to you and says, 'I am sorry' seven times, you must forgive him." Mark 17:3-4.*

I love Mark Twain's definition of forgiveness. He says, "Forgiveness is the fragrance that the violet sheds on the heel that has crushed it." No matter what is said and done to you, just keep loving. Be better than the other person, in that you choose to live aligned with the teachings of Christ instead of giving in to the devil.

Even if the individual does not want to apologise, then you let go nonetheless. You forgive anyhow. I will share with you now three powerful ways that will help you forgive and let go. The first is to find all the benefits of how this situation has served you. There have to be benefits if this has happened to you. You may deny this at first, but if you look closer and deeper, you will find many benefits. What was the lesson in this? How did this serve you? Next meet with the person face to face and openly share how you feel. Do not come together to get into an argument with them, which can result in insulting and blaming. You come together to share your feelings and to close this chapter of your life so that you can move on. Sometimes due to the nature of the relationship, this may not always be possible, and so the best way forward, in this case, would be a write a letter. You can either write a letter to them and email it or write a letter and discard of it. I have written so many letters out of anger but have never hit the send button. I simply needed to release my anger. Thank God I was wise enough not to send my message to them. Just because someone hurts you, does not mean you have to hurt them back even more. *"For if you love only those who love you, what credit is that to you? Even tax collectors do that! And if you exchange greetings only with your own circle, are you doing anything exceptional? Even the pagans do that much. No, you are to be perfect, like your Heavenly Father."* Matthew 5:46-48.

Even your enemies deserve love, and if you can open your heart to forgive and love then, you are becoming more and more like Jesus and our Father. Finally, the third way is by praying about it by speaking to God daily. Ask God to help you let go. I cannot tell you how many times, I have done this and the person actually either apologised or naturally walked away from my life. God's way is always the best way.

Matthew 6:14-15 "For if you forgive other people their failures, your Heavenly Father will also forgive you. But if you will not forgive other people, neither will your Heavenly Father forgive you your failures."

I firmly believe that forgiveness is the key to healing and happiness. Forgive yourself and forgive others and set yourself free. If you can learn to forgive, you will always be at peace. If you are at peace, you will almost always enjoy perfect health.

HEALTH RECORDER
WEEK 11

Monday   Date: _____ **Nº of times**

☐ I have read Chapter 11

☐ I have read the Thought of the Day below

"To be in Love is to be free. If you aren't free on any level, you are not in Love; you are in Fear."

Hitesher Gef

Tuesday   Date: _____ **Nº of times**

☐ I have read Chapter 11

☐ I have read the Thought of the Day below

"My favourite part about loving you is finding new ways to make you smile every day."

Wednesday   Date: _____   **Nº of times**

☐ I have read Chapter 11

☐ I have read the Thought of the Day below

"If you can count the number of good deeds you have done, you have not done enough."

Hitesher Gef

❧

Thursday   Date: _____   **Nº of times**

☐ I have read Chapter 11

☐ I have read the Thought of the Day below

"Instead of crying for yesterday's missed sunset, bath in the magnificence of this morning's sunrise."

Hitesher Gef

❧

Friday   Date: _____   **Nº of times**

☐ I have read Chapter 11

☐ I have read the Thought of the Day below

"Love is the only gift you have, that when you give away, you will actually have more of it."

Hitesher Gef

WEEK 12

HOLY BODY

So far in this book, we have been working on healing at a spiritual, emotional and mental level. I will now share with you how to heal and restore your body to perfect and optimum wellness. If the Kingdom of God is within you and God lives within that kingdom, then this makes your body a temple. *"Do you not know that your bodies are temples of the Holy Spirit, who is in you, whom you have received from God? You are not your own." 1 Corinthians 6:19.*

We spend so much time taking care of our churches, making sure that it is clean and looking beautiful, but how much of this time do we give to the temple of God, which is your body. How much love and respect do we have for this body which we use to do God's work? This body is a precious gift, yet we subject it to so much abuse on a daily basis.

I want to be clear that I am not a medical doctor, a qualified dietician or an alternative health practitioner. The information I am about to share with you is what has worked for me and kept me in perfect health. I have come across this information through years of research/study and by working closely with natural health practitioners. I have been perfectly healthy my whole life. The procedure that I had undergone in the hospital was due to a physical obstruction that needed to be repaired. Further investigation did reveal that this was congenital (I was born with this). Always consult your doctor or nutritionist before making changes to your diet. I must warn you however, that doctors have very little training in nutrition and will tell you that making a change to your diet will have no direct impact on your health.

That is the answer to perfect health; **nutrition**. Whatever you put into your body will determine how healthy you are, how much energy you have, and how much pain you may experience. We are sicker now, than we were 100 years ago. You would think that with the vast advancement in medicine, we would have found remedies and cures for so many diseases. Yet, the opposite is true. People are getting sicker. More people have heart disease, diabetes, high blood pressure, inflammatory diseases and cancer than ever before. It is no mystery as to why this is the case. We simply need to ask ourselves what changed from 100 years ago to today. The answer is: **the food we eat**.

We live fast paced lifestyles that have forced us to live off microwave dinners and fast foods. I have repetitively said that the reason it is called fast food, is because it kills you fast. Using a microwave destroys all the remaining nutrients in your food, and makes your food carcinogenic (cancer causing). These are quite bold claims to make, but if you want to live longer, the first thing to do is get rid of your microwave and heat or cook your food on a stove.

Here are six foods types that you need to stay away from: unnatural sugars, hydrogenated oils, white flour, iodised salt, red meat and milk. If you only avoided these foods, then I guarantee that you will start to reverse your illness.

The next golden rule when it comes to food is to stay away from anything that comes in a packet, a can or a box. You should only eat that which grows on a tree or the ground. The exception to this rule is if what it is in the packet or box contains only 1 or up to 3 ingredients at most. The reason you should avoid anything packaged is that they may contain preservatives. These are deadly toxins which make us sick very slowly. Read the packaging before eating or buying anything. Ignorance is not bliss when it comes to food. Ignorance will hurt you really bad. Here is a list of preservatives that you should definitely avoid: Potassium Bromate, Sulphur Dioxide E220, BHA And BHT E320, Sodium Nitrate, Sodium Sulphite, Food Dyes - E221, E133, E124, E110, E102, Trans Fat, MSG / E621, High Fructose Corn Syrup, Aspartame (found in diet cool drinks) E951.

So what is wrong with fast food? Well, fast food contains hydrogenated oils and lots of sugar. For starters, a can of cool drink has 9 teaspoons of sugar. Do not be fooled into thinking that store bought fruit juices are a healthier alternative. In most cases, store bought fruits juices contain as much sugar as cool drinks and can sometimes contain no fruit juice at all. The companies add pulp to the juice to give you the impression that you are having freshly pressed juice.

The problem with hydrogenated oils is that they contain trans-fat, which raises LDL ("bad") cholesterol, lowers HDL ("good") cholesterol. This means that when you eat food fried in oil; you are quite literally eating a heart attack. Rather cook with coconut oil and use olive oil for dressings. Having refined sugar can shut down your immune system for hours, leaving you vulnerable to getting sick. It can lead to type II diabetes, obesity, can cause liver disease, give you cancer, affect brain function, give you heart disease and is highly addictive. The reason that you can eat so much of chocolate is due to the highly addictive nature of sugar. The first place you can begin to lower your sugar intake is to not have as much tea as you would usually drink, or continue to have your tea but replace your sugar with a little honey, or stevia. Personally, I have my herbal tea without any sugar. It can take a few days to get used to, but my health means more to me than anything else. Be careful of thinking that you may not be having any sugar at all. Sugars are found in canned foods, biscuits and cakes, jams, fruit juices, sauces, yoghurts, and energy drinks. This is just a small list, and you should always remember to read the label. Stay clear of energy drinks if you love your heart, kidney and liver. It hurts me to see parents buying their children energy drinks or even buying it for themselves. Energy drinks are probably one of the most dangerous things that you can put into your body. If you lack energy, then you should rather opt for coconut water, with an apple or banana. I promise you that having these will give you all the energy you need without the side effects and the burn out these drinks give you. If you have a problem with your kidneys, then you should not have too much of coconut water and bananas as they contain high levels of potassium.

White flour is the colour white because the wheat (germ and bran) has been bleached by a substance called Alloxan, which destroy the beta cells in your pancreas, which can result in diabetes. White flour also contains a substance called gluten, which can lead to you having leaky gut syndrome, IBS, and other digestive problems. White flour is highly processed and contains almost no nutritional value. Avoid bread as much as possible and if you have to have it, rather opt for rye bread. I personally also avoid white rice. My alternatives to bread and white rice are brown basmati rice, quinoa, whole brown rice, millet, and buckwheat.

We have too much of salt in our diet. This is particularly the case with iodised salt. This salt can raise your blood pressure which can lead to strokes, heart disease, and kidney disease. A safer alternative is Himalayan salt or sea salt.

Milk is not what is used to be. Nowadays, milk is highly pasteurized and contains hormones, antibiotics, pesticides and other drugs that are unfit for human consumption. Further to this milk does not contain as much calcium as we are actually told. Milk is also acidic and can lead to gas and exacerbates acne. If you suffer from sinuses or post nasal drip, then you should stay clear of milk as it creates an excess of mucus and causes inflammation in the body. Besides this, cow's milk is for a calf, not human beings. It contains everything that a baby cow needs. You are not a baby cow. Alternate sources of calcium are kale and other green vegetables, almonds, kidney beans and chickpeas.

If you want to have meat, I would suggest sticking to white meat such as chicken and fish. Red meat contains hormones that have been injected into the animal to speed up its growth. It also hardens blood vessels and contains saturated fat which raises your cholesterol. Meat should be cooked well. The idea of having meat rare puts you at risk for bacterial, viral and parasite infection. I think above all of this, we don't know what we are getting in our meat today. The meat is mixed with all sorts of animals and put together with harmful chemicals that can make you even sicker.

Without going into a debate on Genetically Modified Food here, I will just share with you that food that has been modified to resist pests/insects and natural weather conditions contain chemicals that can only do more harm than good to your body. Anything that is labelled as GMO should be avoided at all costs. In most cases, it is our corn that is modified and can be hidden in chips or crisps. This is all I want to say on GMO's in this book.

All of the above can be summarized in one simple sentence. Eat real food that comes from God's Grocery. In other words, eat fresh food and vegetable and eat white meat that comes from a reputable source.

Disease is experienced in the body when we poison it with toxins, when we create an acidic environment by overindulging in the foods above, and whenever there is any inflamma-tion in the body. In order to repair the body, we have to begin by removing our habits that are damaging the body. There are a lot more that I cannot cover right now because it does not fit into the vision of this book. I have a 4-hour workshop where I teach people the exact cause of disease with remedies, how to live perfectly healthy lives, which includes providing informa-tion on how to prepare food, the correct foods to eat, and what superfoods and nutrients are needed for the body so that you remain pain and disease free. I believe that God intended for us to live healthy and happy lives. If you are interested in this workshop, please send an email to support@livebyfaith.co.za and I would be glad to send you more information.

As a gift from me to you, please email support@livebyfaith.co.za for a complimentary health assessment by one of the expert health consultants. Use the words "God is my Healer" in your subject line to receive this session. May you always be blessed with perfect health.

HEALTH RECORDER
WEEK 12

Monday   Date: _____   **Nº of times** [ ]

☐ I have read Chapter 12
☐ I have read the Thought of the Day below

"Knowledge is knowing when to say yes. True wisdom is having the courage to say 'No' when it's time to."

Hitesher Gef

Tuesday   Date: _____   **Nº of times** [ ]

☐ I have read Chapter 12
☐ I have read the Thought of the Day below

"Studies show that walking significantly improves your health. You should try walking away and notice how much your entire life improves!"

Hitesher Gef

Wednesday   Date: _____   **N° of times**

☐ I have read Chapter 12

☐ I have read the Thought of the Day below

"You can never be in 2 places at the same time. If you fit IN, then you definitely can't stand OUT."

Hitesher Gef

Thursday   Date: _____   **N° of times**

☐ I have read Chapter 12

☐ I have read the Thought of the Day below

"The most beautiful people I have met on the planet are the ones that have chosen to honour their authenticity."

Hitesher Gef

Friday   Date: _____   **N° of times**

☐ I have read Chapter 12

☐ I have read the Thought of the Day below

"The most beautiful things in the world are not the shiny things. The most beautiful, are the things that allow you to shine in the world."

Hitesher Gef

WALK BY FAITH

God bless you for completing the **12 Weeks of Healing through CHRIST** programme. I have faith that you are at least one step closer to experiencing good health and wellness. Keep reading this book if you have to, to keep your faith strong. Never stop praying and believe that you will be healed.

I know that God will never let his followers down and will take of you. I will personally keep praying for you daily, as I do for all my family and friends.

God loves you. Rest and be at peace in His love. Your miracle is on its way.

God bless you always.

If you found value and healing through this book and want to make a copy available to someone else, then go to **livebyfaith.co.za** and donate a copy of this book for them. We will print a copy and make it available to those who cannot afford it, as we travel across the globe. Remember that a percentage of this book goes towards a charity/charities mentioned on our website.

PAY IT FORWARD

You can also Pay it Forward by distributing 10 copies of this book to your family and friends after you have completed the book and found healing for yourself. If it is healing that you seek for yourself, then go out and support others find healing for themselves. Whatever we do for others, we always receive in return a thousand fold. For more information visit **livebyfaith.co.za**

NOTES

NOTES

NOTES

www.ingramcontent.com/pod-product-compliance
Lightning Source LLC
Chambersburg PA
CBHW070642030426
42337CB00020B/4130